IMAGES
of America

GREGORY AND CHARLES
MIX COUNTIES

The railroad was instrumental in the settling of both Gregory and Charles Mix Counties. Numerous towns sprang up along the railroad route and depended on the railroad for their survival. Mr. McCants, son Bill, and Eldrid Heffern converse in front of the water supply tank at the Herrick depot. The trains needed to take on water about every eight to ten miles, necessitating frequent stops along the track. (Courtesy Herrick News Subscribers.)

IMAGES
of America

GREGORY AND CHARLES
MIX COUNTIES

Jan Cerney

ARCADIA
PUBLISHING

Published by Arcadia Publishing
Charleston, South Carolina

Library of Congress Catalog Card Number: 2004107877

For all general information contact Arcadia Publishing at:
Telephone 843-853-2070
Fax 843-853-0044
E-mail sales@arcadiapublishing.com
For customer service and orders:
Toll-Free 1-888-313-2665

Visit us on the Internet at www.arcadiapublishing.com

Both Gregory and Charles Mix Counties were primarily agricultural communities. The invention of the tractor revolutionized agriculture. These farmers pose with their new labor saving machinery. (Courtesy Charles Mix County Historical Society.)

CONTENTS

ACKNOWLEDGMENTS

My search for photographs documenting the area's history led me from the beaten path, back into the heart of each community. Many towns that once flourished during the land rush days have dwindled in size or disappeared from the scene. The hustle and bustle of an earlier time has been replaced with active families valuing the small town life. The quiet Main Streets, while reduced in number of businesses, still cater to their citizens.

A sense of community pride shines through the restoration projects, museums, schools, and traditional celebrations that each community holds dear.

I feel fortunate to have been able to visit each nook and cranny and meet with the people who have provided photographs and information along with their gracious western hospitality. Thank you to the following individuals: Ruth Malone, Richard Rubel, Betty Shaffer, Kathy Devine, Dianne King, Alis Veren, Dick Kafka, Janet Ticknor, Mark Gau, Bill White, Richard Papousek, and others who have provided photos.

I dedicate this book to all my relatives who settled in both counties and to my husband's relatives who settled in Gregory County. To his family, the Cerneys and the Pochops, and to my family, the Broziks, who homesteaded in Gregory County. To my Grandma and Grandpa Bouska who owned a shoe repair shop in Gregory for many years after living in Wagner for a time and to other Bouska relatives who resided in Charles Mix County.

America was on the move to the land rush on the Rosebud. Since Bonesteel was the terminus for the railroad, it became the gateway to the Rosebud. A record 106,296 people registered for the much sought after land that would be parceled out in lottery fashion. Only one in 2,600 would have their number drawn. A carnival atmosphere pervaded the town, accentuated by a lawless element. (Courtesy Andrew Qualm Collection.)

INTRODUCTION

The history of Gregory and Charles Mix Counties has been influenced by their geographical locations as well as western military and government policies. The Arikara Indians, among the first inhabitants, built their earthen lodges along the Missouri River, the counties' shared border. The Arikara eventually succumbed to the white man's diseases and the constant harassment of the Teton Sioux who migrated from Minnesota and crossed west of the Missouri River in 1750. With the acquisition of the horse, the Sioux became dominant over the western plains for the next 100 years.

In the late 1850s, white settlement had advanced east of the Missouri River with sights set on land now occupied by the Yankton Sioux. The Yanktons were pressured to relinquish their hold on the area. Realizing they lacked the strength to resist white encroachment, they signed a treaty in 1858 agreeing to withdraw to a reservation along the Missouri River in present day Charles Mix County. The tribe was to receive annuities of $1.6 million over a 50 year period. In July 1859, white settlers began to occupy the ceded land while the Yankton Sioux left for the Greenwood Agency.

When the white man began crossing the Indian Territory to the gold fields of California and Montana, the Teton Sioux rebelled against the intrusion into their country. Sioux unrest and earlier treaty obligations necessitated the construction of forts along the Missouri. Fort Randall was one such fort constructed in 1856 to keep the peace and distribute annuities. The signing of the Fort Laramie Treaty in 1868 set aside the Great Sioux Reservation for the Sioux in western South Dakota. Non-Indians were not allowed on the reservations except for government employees and officials. The treaty helped to stabilize Indian and white relationships for a time until the Custer Expedition announced to the world that gold had been discovered in the Black Hills in 1874.

The public clamored for government purchase of the Black Hills while they were trespassing on the land in search of gold. Eventually in 1877, the Hills were acquired and later, the reservation further divided into six smaller reservations: The Brule, Standing Rock, Cheyenne River, Crow Creek, Pine Ridge, and the Rosebud. The Allotment Act was passed in 1887 further dividing the land into 160-acre parcels for each Indian family.

In 1904, surplus Rosebud Reservation land was thrown open to settlement in Gregory County. To avoid the land rushes of former years in states like Oklahoma, a lottery system was used to sell 160-acre plots. Land seekers flocked to the registrations points, including Bonesteel and Fairfax, to register for the drawing. Bonesteel attracted its share of thugs, crooks, and opportunists that turned it into a lawless town. The Battle of Bonesteel resulted when law-abiding citizens drove out the undesirable elements.

When the drawings concluded, the lucky winners began to build their homesteads. The cattle empires withered due in part to the advance of the homesteaders into range country. The railroad laid their tracks, linking the area to the outside world. The Indians, relegated to reservations, attempted to adapt to a changing world. The broken prairie yielded to productive crops during the good years, but these years were interspersed with dry weather cycles. The new settlers learned dry land farming methods and prospered in spite of the setbacks. The decade of the 1930s brought the most difficult challenge that the farmers ever had to face. Constant dry conditions and dust storms drove many off their land to regions of more promise. Those that could survive rejoiced when rain finally returned to the county in the 1940s.

The Pick-Sloan Plan of 1944 authorized the building of four rolled-earth dams on the Missouri River in South Dakota to develop irrigation, provide electrical power, control flooding, create recreational opportunities, and enhance navigation. The Fort Randall Dam was the first to be built. After 10 years of construction, the dam was dedicated in August 1956.

This book is just a sampling of the history and events of Gregory and Charles Mix Counties. It is not meant to be a comprehensive history; therefore, not all communities have been included. Photographs were not readily available for certain areas, making it difficult for their inclusion. Nonetheless, the beauty, the spirit, and the lasting legacy of both counties will shine through for future generations.

Wagner's elevators tower over the railroad tracks. Grain elevators were a trademark of the Midwest. Their ubiquitous presence dominated each town's landscape as a testament to the productivity of the land as well as the hard work and dedication of its people. (Courtesy Charles Mix County Historical Society.)

One

COUNCIL FIRES

The Sioux rove and follow the buffalo, raise no corn or anything else, the woods and prairies affording a sufficiency. They eat meat, and substitute the ground potato, which grows on the plains, for bread.

—Journals of Lewis and Clark

Named the Sioux by the French, the plains tribes consisted of the Seven Council Fires. The Santee Sioux were the Dakota, the Yankton Sioux, the Nakota, and the Lakota were the Teton Sioux. This group of Lakotas is pictured in Dallas during a celebration. (Courtesy Gregory County Historical Society.)

The Yankton Sioux lived in the timber country of Minnesota before moving into South Dakota's James River Valley. In Minnesota, they lived in wigwams constructed of poles, earth, and bark. After moving to South Dakota, they became nomadic and lived in teepees made of animal skins. They subsisted on the buffalo and traded with the Arikara for agricultural products. (Courtesy Charles Mix County Historical Society.)

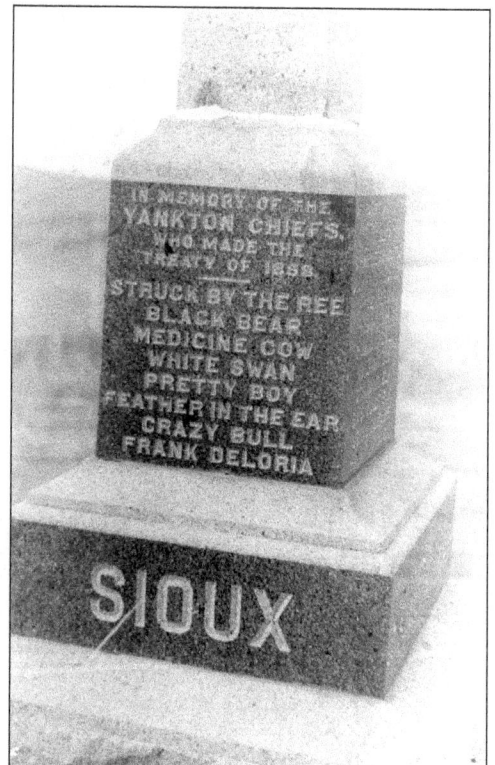

A monument was erected in memory of the Yankton Chiefs who signed the 1858 treaty ceding their lands. The treaty created the first South Dakota Indian Reservation known as the Yankton Agency and later called Greenwood. (Courtesy Charles Mix County Historical Society.)

Chief Strike the Ree, known also as Struck By the Ree, realized that the Yankton Sioux were no match for the encroaching white man and encouraged a peaceful negotiation of the 1858 treaty. Legend tells a story that Lewis and Clark wrapped the then baby Struck by the Ree in an American flag on their famous expedition as a sign of friendship. Struck by the Ree became a friend of the white man as well as a chief. He flew an American flag every day at the Greenwood Agency. The flagpole that he used still stands. (Courtesy South Dakota Historical Society State Archives and The Smithsonian.)

Guests enjoy the porch of the Greenwood Hotel, which was built to house agents. Some of the other buildings located at the agency included officers' buildings, storage tank, warehouse, Williamson home, grist mill, saw mill, the mission and women's missionary society house. (Courtesy Charles Mix County Historical Society.)

Major Daniels, superintendent of the Greenwood Agency, was a Civil War veteran. Many Civil War veterans migrated west to join the military. The agencies' role was to introduce the Sioux to agriculture, education, white religion, and to the white man's way of life. Some of the Yanktons practiced farming and raised corn. They built log houses and barns for their livestock. (Charles Mix County Historical Society.)

Rev. John Poage Williamson ministered to the Yankton Sioux at the Greenwood Agency in 1869. He built his first church from logs under protest from the Yanktons. Later the brick Presbyterian Church was built in 1914. (Courtesy Charles Mix County Historical Society.)

Eighteen-year-old Emma Spider,
a Yankton Sioux, probably of the
Greenwood Agency, poses for a
picture. (Courtesy Charles Mix County
Historical Society.)

The building to the left, St. John's Catholic Mission, was established in 1914. Rev. Henry Westropp of St. Francis came to Marty Mission in 1913 to preach. He built St. John the Apostle Church in Greenwood. President Grant had issued a proclamation in 1869 that only one denomination could work within an agency. The Presbyterians were the first to minister at Greenwood. The Catholics were allowed to do so in 1913. (Courtesy Charles Mix County Historical Society.)

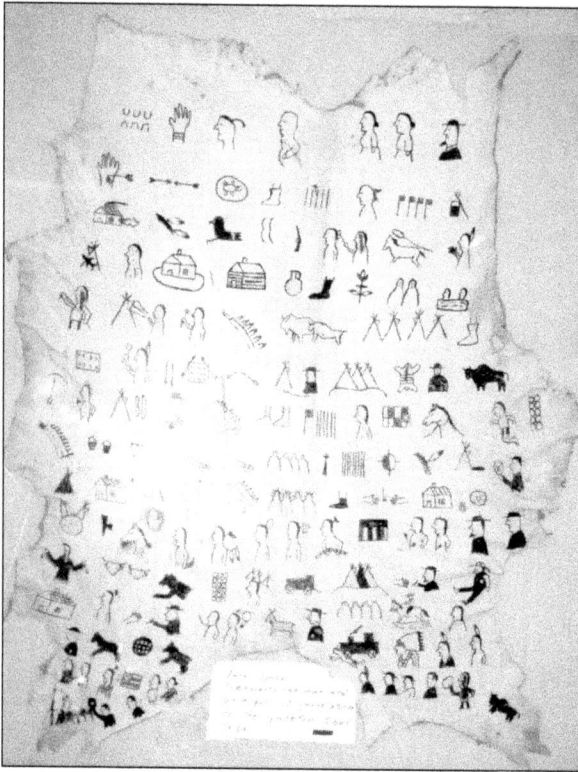

This winter count made of deerskin and painted with symbols is displayed in the Charles Mix County Museum in Wagner. The Sioux recorded a pictorial record of the past by using winter counts. Usually they were painted in a spiral form with the first year starting in the center. Each symbol represents one year and an event of importance to the Yankton Sioux.

A close up view of the winter count shows the symbols in more detail. The spotted bodies denote the great smallpox epidemic of 1837–1838 and the log cabins and priests symbolize the transition to reservation life. The museum has a written translation of each symbol.

14

When the Indian chiefs would visit Washington as a delegation, they were given suits, coats, and shiny black shoes to wear. Oftentimes the chiefs would cover their detested garb with the more familiar Indian blankets. (Courtesy Charles Mix County Historical Society.)

This Yankton Sioux Chief poses in his more familiar native dress against a backdrop of the nation's capitol. (Courtesy Charles Mix County Historical Society.)

Lewis and Clark noted the presence of the Ponca Indians along the mouth of Ponca Creek. The Ponca traded with Europeans beginning the last decade of the eighteenth century. The peaceful Ponca farmed along the creek near the Niobrara region. Pictured is an Indian agent with Ponca Chiefs. (Courtesy South Dakota State Historical Society State Archives; Morrow Collection.)

The village of White Swan, existing from 1869–1895, was named after Chief Swan of the Yankton Sioux and was located across the Missouri River from Fort Randall. The village was comprised of agency workers, merchants, and civilians who worked at Fort Randall as well as Indians who chose to live with the whites. White Swan was a way station for stagecoaches that ran from Sioux City and Yankton to White Swan. (Courtesy Charles Mix Country Historical Society.)

16

When living in the agencies the Sioux were entirely dependent on the government for food and clothing. Cattle for beef rations were driven to the camp where they were turned loose. The Indians hunted them down and butchered them as if they were buffalo using arrows and bullets. The men in the photo are wearing felt hats and clothing from Government Issue. (Courtesy Badlands National Park, Interior; John A. Anderson photo.)

Sinte Gleska, a Brule Chief, was named Spotted Tail for the raccoon tail that he wore as a talisman in battle. Spotted Tail possessed unusual abilities in dealing the government concerning his people. He worked for peaceful relations between the Brule and the government, realizing opposition would be futile for them. Colonel Mills described him as a handsome man, fine looking and with engaging manners. Photo c. 1877. (Courtesy Badlands National Park, Interior and The Smithsonian.)

Spotted Tail lived for a time in the White River County. When game grew scarce, the Brule moved to the Platte River area. After the Fort Laramie Treaty of 1868, the Brule were moved to the Whetstone Agency, 23 miles above Fort Randall. Spotted Tail disliked it there because of the whiskey trade. His people moved five times before the Rosebud Agency was established on Rosebud Creek in 1878. (Courtesy Badlands National Park, Interior and The Smithsonian.)

The Sioux held powwows often where they celebrated their traditions with dancing. A group of drummers and singers, appearing to the right of the photo, provide the drumbeats. (Courtesy Badlands National Park, Interior.)

The government furnished a day school and boarding facility near Dixon for the Sioux Indians. The school was built near running springs, which supplied water for the school. The rock building housed the springs for the water supply. The school was situated between Little Bijou Hills on the north and the Nogi Buttes on the south. In addition to the school, there was a residence for teachers and 40 to 50 log homes where Indian families could live while their children attended school. The Sioux did some farming while living there and put up hay for their horses. Photo c. 1895. (Courtesy Betty Shaffer.)

Children are in attendance at the Indian Day School near Dixon. Attendance was compulsory. Missionaries and priests devoted their lives to educating and helping the Indian people to adjust to their new way of life. (Courtesy Richard Papousek.)

An old Episcopal cemetery near the former Dixon Indian School contains markers and graves of early Sioux residents in the area. The gravestone that towers above the rest belongs to Chief Tatankawakan also known as Medicine Bull, an important Brule Chief. (Courtesy Betty Shaffer.)

A portion of the gravestone with Chief Tatankawkan's name gives his birth as 1825 and death as 1906. He signed five treaties when he was chief, and they are listed on the stone as well. One that he signed is the Fort Laramie Treaty of 1868 that created the Great Sioux Indian Reservation west of the Missouri River. (Courtesy Betty Shaffer.)

Two main Indian settlements existed in Gregory County. One was with Chief Milk in the southern part of the county and the other in the northwest was under the leadership of the Brule Chief Medicine Bull, who is pictured. (Courtesy South Dakota State Historical Society State Archives and The Smithsonian.)

Darrell McCollam stands between the two graves of Mary Red Horse and her husband in the old Indian cemetery. Someone vandalized the pictures of the deceased that were encased in the oval frames. (Courtesy Betty Shaffer.)

Swift Bear was a Dakota Brule delegate to Washington in 1872. When the Great Sioux Reservation was divided into smaller reservations in 1889, Swift Bear and his Brule lived for a time on Whetstone Agency where they attempted to comply with government policy and become agriculturalists. Eventually Swift Bear and his corn band moved to camp on the Ponca south of Burke. (Courtesy South Dakota State Historical Society Archives and The Smithsonian.)

Two

FORT RANDALL

We get plenty to eat and more than we can eat. We have Beefe three days in the week and pork four days. When we have pork we have rice in our soupe; when we have Beefe we have beans. . . .

—Amos Cherry

Fort Randall was built in 1856 of logs and named for Daniel Randall, Deputy Paymaster of the U.S. Army. The fort was established to maintain peace with the Sioux and protect the travelers as well as distribute annuities as set forth in the treaties. During the gold fever of 1875, soldiers were required to keep illegal gold seekers off the Indians land. In the 1880s the fort became a supply depot. (Courtesy U.S. Army Corps of Engineers.)

Fort Randall looks north in this 1860 photograph. By 1871, the old fort was in a state of decay. Frame buildings replaced the old log structures at a cost of $20,000. The new buildings were built directly over the old. The cantonment, or fort, was constructed of buildings surrounding the parade ground. There was no stockade. (Courtesy U.S. Army Corps of Engineers.)

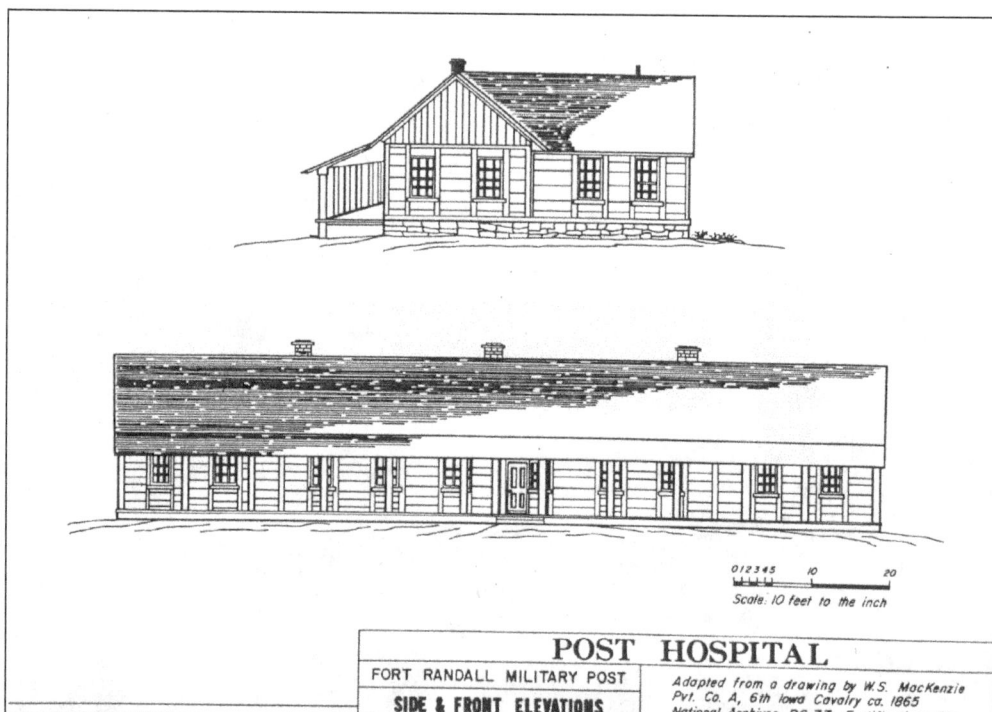

012345   10   20
Scale: 10 feet to the inch

POST HOSPITAL

FORT RANDALL MILITARY POST	Adapted from a drawing by W.S. MacKenzie
SIDE & FRONT ELEVATIONS	Pvt. Co. A, 6th Iowa Cavalry ca. 1865
	National Archives, RG 77, Fortifications File

This sketch was adapted from a drawing by Private W.S. Mackenzie of the post hospital in 1865. Colonel Sackett described the hospital in an 1866 report. "The location of hospital is good, ventilation is bad—It has three wards—room enough for 8 to 10 beds in each ward. It is filled as every other building with bedbugs, fleas, etc.—Water is hauled from river. Well water is alkaline." (Courtesy U.S. Army Corps of Engineers.)

Another post hospital was built in 1872 and contained enough room for 24 patients. The post also had an infirmary and a horse drawn ambulance. Among the post surgeons and physicians at the post were Dr. Slaughter, Dr. Jon Campbell, Dr. Cambrud, and Dr. Gorgas. Dr. Gorgas later helped to combat yellow fever during the construction of the Panama Canal. He treated both settlers and Indians while he served at the fort. (Courtesy U.S. Army Corps of Engineers.)

Approximately 2,000 soldiers occupied Fort Randall. In the early years, soldiers found Fort Randall to be desolate and monotonous. Desertions were common. The fort organized more social activities to keep the soldiers involved. Fraternal societies, military balls, picnics, masquerades, sleighing parties, dramatics, and band concerts were encouraged. (Courtesy U.S. Army Corps of Engineers.)

In 1875, soldiers of Fort Randall, who were members of the I.O.O.F. Lodge, embarked on a private endeavor to build a lodge, which would also house a library and a church. George Bush, a discharged soldier and post carpenter, designed the building to be made from hand-sawn chalkstone from nearby quarries. The left side of the chapel contained the church, the center the Mason's meeting hall, and the library occupied the right, containing 1,500 volumes. The church design and fixtures were constructed of polished walnut and the finest glass and metal. The pulpit revolved to accommodate either Catholic or Protestant services. Hot water pipes beneath the floor heated the rooms. (Courtesy Dick Kafka.)

Mostly native materials were used in the chapel's construction. Cottonwood, red wood, and pine from nearby groves were sawed into lumber at the post's sawmill. Bricks were made in the brick factory. Black walnut was transported from the East. Stained glass was used in the arched windows. No nails were used in the construction. Windstorms and a lightning bolt wrecked havoc with the chapel. (Courtesy Gregory County Historical Society.)

The Corps of Engineers stabilized the remaining structure in 1953. Now only memories haunt the ruins of the chapel. One such memory was the wedding of Miss Mattie Lugenbeel and S.H. Gruber in 1879. (U.S. Army Corps of Engineers.)

The ruins of the post chapel nestle in the trees with the Missouri River in the background. (Courtesy U.S. Army Corps of Engineers.)

The Corps of Engineers added a roof in 2003 for the protection and stabilization of the chapel.

The former elegance of the bell tower, the leaded stained glass windows, the high arched ceiling with walnut beams, and the ornamental designs of European influence can only now be imagined.

This 1879 photo is of the Commanders Officers' House. The officers of the 25th Infantry were stationed here. (Courtesy U.S. Army Corps of Engineers.)

The Headquarters Building's framework was made from cedar logs and sided over with materials brought from St. Louis in about 1855. The building had 16 rooms. McLaughlin and Ed A. Fry stand to the right of the photo. McLaughlin served as custodian of Fort Randall after it was abandoned. Fry edited the Lake Andes *Wave* at that time. (Courtesy U.S. Army Corps of Engineers.)

The post Commanders House was one of the buildings left at Fort Randall. It was known as the McLaughlin house in 1915. In its early days, it was referred to as "the house" and became the focal point of the parade ground. After the fort's abandonment, the headquarters became a farmhouse and a post office. In 1929, a farmhand was cooking and left the damper on the stove closed causing a fire that destroyed the house. (Courtesy U.S. Army Corps of Engineers.)

These soldiers wait for battalion inspection. Pass in review would occur each Sunday on the parade ground and was symbolic of the military routine. (Courtesy U.S. Army Corps of Engineers.)

The 15th Infantry, officers and soldiers stand in front of the soldiers' barracks. Many types of soldiers came to the frontier. Many nationalities joined the local boys. Volunteer companies kept the fort manned during battles. A few confederate troops escaping prison, called Galvanized Yankees, came to the frontier. Soldiers of African descent were known as the Buffalo Soldiers because their hair resembled the buffalo. (Courtesy U.S. Army Corps of Engineers.)

31

Standing at attention is Company A, 15th Co. Infantry. In 1891, the 21st Infantry replaced the 15th Infantry. One-year later, Fort Randall was discontinued as a military post. (Courtesy U.S. Army Corps of Engineers.)

The infantry target practice in this 1890 photo. The 40-70 Springfield rifle was one of the earliest breech loading rifles to be manufactured in large quantities. It was the standard weapon for the U.S. Army troops from 1870-1890. (Courtesy U.S. Army Corps of Engineers.)

This 1880 photo is of post children attending the Fort Randall School. Pictured here, from left to right, seated, are: Mollie or Nellie Reider, Lizzie Reider, Katie Cassidy, Ada Reynolds, Mary Master, Louise Moran, Frank, Antonie and James Herman, Pharris Glick, Edward Cassidy, John and Taylor Glick; back row: John Scherer, John Cassidy, Jack Moran, Andrew Cassidy, Franz Scherer, Carl Reider, George Reynolds, and base teacher Dr. Caulkin. (Courtesy U.S. Army Corps of Engineers.)

The Officers' Duplex in 1882 accommodated the married officers. Rock-lined cellars were built under these buildings. White picket fences enclosed all buildings and yards and were kept in impeccable repair. (Courtesy U.S. Army Corps of Engineers.)

The unidentified officers served in various capacities at Fort Randall. Here on the frontier, officers and their families enjoyed relative wealth and high standing. Archaeologists have uncovered gilt-edged china, ivory buttons, and fragments of porcelain dolls at their living quarter sites. (Courtesy U.S. Army Corps of Engineers.)

This last military formation at Fort Randall was held in 1892. The flag flown that day is preserved at West Point Military Academy. The fort's buildings were auctioned off, moved, or dismantled. Two houses remained as residences. (Courtesy U.S. Army Corps of Engineers.)

In 1872, Buffalo Bill Cody visited Fort Randall while scouting for a McPherson Calvary unit. Later in 1881, Fort Randall placed Sitting Bull under surveillance. Visitors flocked to the fort to see the famous Hunkpapa chief and have their pictures taken with him. The above photo, dated 1885, was taken by David Notman of Sitting Bull's only tour with Cody's Wild West Show. (Courtesy Badlands National Park, Interior and The Smithsonian.)

The passage of time has worn away the inscriptions on Jacob Herman's headstone in the Fort Randall Post Cemetery. In 1892, the post cemetery record listed 138 men and civilians buried in the graveyard. The first 21 were listed as unknown.

The headstone marks the grave of a year-old boy, Oliver Shannon Pratt born in 1881, died in 1882. In 1893, 67 individuals in the cemetery were removed and re-interred at Fort Leavenworth, Kansas. An additional 16 unknowns buried at the post cemetery were removed from a burial site in 1952 which lies covered by the reservoir. Four other unrecorded gravesites are known to exist within the cemetery.

Sitting Bull and his family are under guard of the 25th Infantry at Ft. Randall. The Canadian authorities turned him and 154 members of his tribe over to the Infantry. Captain Bentzon is mounted in the picture. The woman in the hat has not been identified. (Courtesy South Dakota State Historical Society State Archives.)

Three

TOWNS OF
CHARLES MIX

*There are certain things concrete in the future growth of a prairie town; the first is it has a railroad;
the next is agricultural territory . . . and last, are the business men of the town.*

–Oscar Micheaux

In 1857, Cuthbert Ducharme, a French trapper, also known as Papineau, opened a store and trading post at Papineau Springs, two miles east of Wheeler. He dealt in whiskey and traded for furs. His customers were Indians, fur trappers, soldiers, and settlers. In 1862, the Papineau Trading Post was designated the county seat of Charles Mix County.

On August 10, 1972, the Papineau post was moved from near the Missouri River to Geddes. The town citizens re-sided the building's log exterior with lap siding. The headstones of the nearby post cemetery were also moved. The remains were re-interred elsewhere.

A colony of Hollanders settled Platte in 1882. The town was named for Platte Creek. Several years later, autos were such a novelty that they were often included in celebrations and parades. (Courtesy Lewis VanderBoom.)

John Bartoco, in the dark suit, set up a tent in Platte to sell his cars. He later built the building now known as the Creamery to sell his automobiles. In the early 1930s, the building was converted to a creamery business. That building was sold again in 1979. (Courtesy Lewis VanderBoom.)

Horses pull a Fresno in constructing Lake Platte. The man in white is Bill Boland. (Courtesy Lewis VanderBoom.)

Workers with their teams and their horse drawn equipment set out to create Lake Platte. (Courtesy Lewis VanderBoom.)

Geddes, a railroad boomtown, was established in 1900. The town suffered fires and tornadoes and growth ceased in 1920. Geddes is now home to the Papineau Trading Post, which was moved from the Missouri when the post was threatened with flooding from the construction of Fort Randall dam. Peter Norbeck's boyhood home is located in Geddes also. (Courtesy Charles Mix County Historical Society.)

This was Wagner's Main Street in 1918. Wagner, a railroad town, was established in 1896, three and one half miles from its present location. It was called Tesapana, or "Tarpaper Town." The population of Wagner grew from 1900 to 1907 with an influx of immigrants from Sweden, Holland, Norway, and Bohemia. (Courtesy Charles Mix County Historical Society.)

Mabel Bullock, daughter of Mr. and Mrs. George Bullock was the first white child born in Wagner in 1900. She stands next to an interesting home on wheels. (Courtesy Charles Mix County Historical Society.)

Frank Rochelle, Frank Paton, Mr. Miller, Art Danke, Miss Safety, and Bill Denoma stand in front of a 1909 Wagner store. (Courtesy Charles Mix County Historical Society.)

This series of six-grain elevators in the 1910 photo was called Elevator Row in Wagner. The depot appears to the right. (Courtesy Charles Mix County Historical Society.)

I.G. Hall unloads goods from the refrigerated railroad car for delivery at the Wagner stores. (Courtesy Charles Mix County Historical Society.)

Henry Bucholz and Dave Bucholz, on the horse, appear in front of Wagner's livery barn. (Courtesy Charles Mix County Historical Society.)

The type of railroad locomotive assigned to the Napa-Platte line was commonly known as a ten-wheeler, four pilot, and six driving wheels. This type was first introduced on the Milwaukee Road early in the 1880s. The Milwaukee Railroad had 500 of them in service at one time. (Courtesy Charles Mix County Historical Society.)

On October 14, 1914, workers began to build the Washington Memorial Highway through Wagner. (Courtesy Charles Mix County Historical Society.)

Bill Wolfe delivered mail near Wagner by horse and buggy. (Courtesy Charles Mix Historical Society.)

Either Bill Wolfe or Bert Gillette delivers U.S. mail on the Star Route serving Smithland and Rodney. (Courtesy Charles Mix Historical Society.)

An attractive window display appears in T.G. Hall's Cooperative Store in Wagner. (Courtesy Charles Mix County Historical Society.)

Ralph James and Harvey Wheeler stand next to a supply of feed sacks in the R.N. Feed Store located on the corner of Main and First Streets in Wagner. It later became the Anderson Building where the business bought eggs, chickens, and cream. (Courtesy Charles Mix County Historical Society.)

46

The J.H. Queal and Company Lumberyard later became the United Building Center in Wagner. Frank N. Nider was the manager and Ron Dilts was the assistant. (Charles Mix County Historical Society.)

A group of people cut ice on the Missouri River in 1922. The cut blocks would then be taken to ice houses for storage until it became necessary to cool the iceboxes used for refrigeration. (Courtesy Charles Mix County Historical Society.)

A 1930 oil well near Wagner yielded no oil but provided enough natural gas to be piped to an area farm. (Courtesy Charles Mix County Historical Society.)

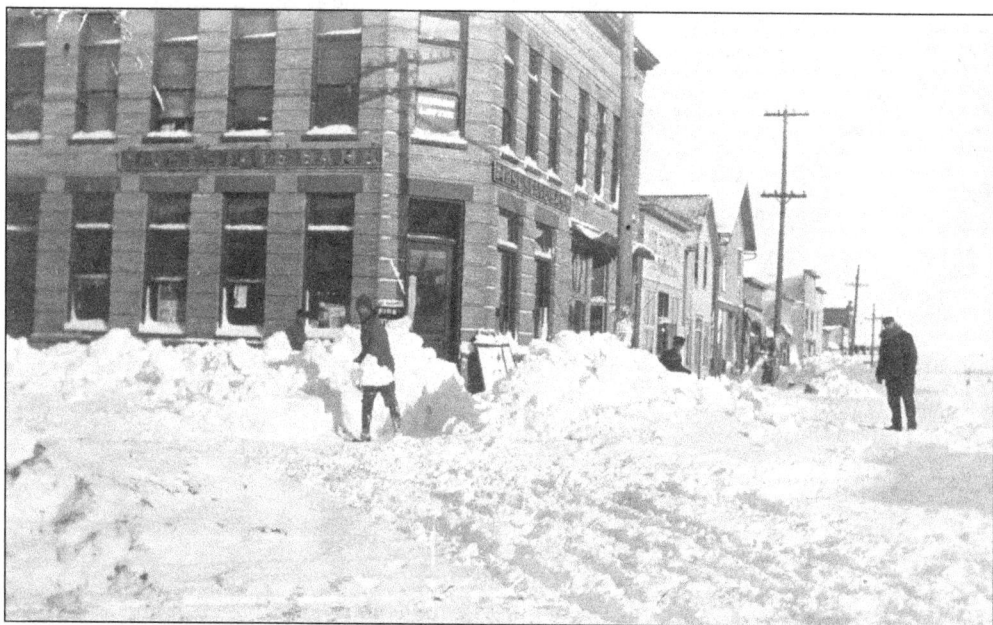

Residents scoop snow in Wagner in 1949 or 1950. (Courtesy Charles Mix County Historical Society.)

Another railroad town, Dante, was platted on April 5, 1907. The depot was built in the same year in which the railroad extended its line from Yankton to Wagner, Geddes, and Platte. (Courtesy Charles Mix County Historical Society.)

Pictured is the 1911 Dante pool hall and meat market. The pool hall belonged to owner Albert Milmer Sr. and Joseph Melmer owned the Dante Meat Market. (Courtesy Charles Mix County Historical Society.)

Lakes Andes was established in 1904 and was named for the nearby lake. At first the lake was named Handy's Lake for an early fur trapper but later became known as Lake Andes. In 1936, the Lake Andes National Wildlife Refuge was established. The 12-mile long lake is a popular fishing and hunting resort. (Courtesy South Dakota State Historical Society State Archives.)

Rest Haven, a popular spot on Friday night, especially during the 1930s and 1940s, hosted dance bands to play in its dance halls. Cabins and a café were also on the resort site at Lake Andes. In the summer of 1984, the building burned down. Well-known bands and performers, including Lawrence Welk, played at Rest Haven. (Courtesy Charles Mix County Historical Society.)

Another view of Rest Haven Resort spouts artesian water in the foreground. In 1922, this new Rest Haven replaced the original Rest Haven destroyed by a cyclone in July 1922. (Courtesy Charles Mix County Historical Society.)

The three men, Henry Timm, Charles Ahrens, and John Timm display their catch from Lake Andes. The photo is entitled "A Sleepless Night." (Courtesy Charles Mix County Historical Society.)

In 1916, Lake Andes won the county seat. Wheeler had been the county seat prior to Lake Andes. In 1917, a courthouse, costing $150,000 was built on a rise on the east end of town. (Courtesy South Dakota State Historical Society State Archives.)

ROSEBUD BRIDGE—MISSOURI RIVER
SOUTH DAKOTA

On January 30, 1953, contractors began tearing down the Rosebud Bridge, also known as the Wheeler Bridge at a cost of $1,285,832 for a move to Chamberlain. The bridge, dedicated in 1923, accommodated traffic on U.S. 18 and 281. Prior to the construction of the bridge, ferries transported people and supplies between Gregory and Charles Mix Counties. After removal of the Rosebud Bridge, traffic was diverted across the Fort Randall Dam. (Courtesy Charles Mix County Historical Society.)

Four

TOWNS OF
GREGORY COUNTY

I remember . . . the sound of a town alive and vibrant with business. The sounds of teams and wagons coming to and from town, the old cars chugging and complaining up the streets, and on a quiet summer morn, the pealing of church bells calling people to mass.

–George Peabody

Established in 1892, Fairfax has the distinction of being the oldest town in Gregory County and the first county seat. In 1890, the Sioux ceded a narrow strip of land in Gregory County bordering the Missouri River. The strip extended south to Nebraska, two miles west of Bonesteel and north to the Missouri River. The people who settled on this land were called squatters. (Courtesy Gregory County Historical Society.)

With the arrival of the Verdigre, Nebraska branch of the railroad in 1902, Fairfax prospered and many businesses were formed. Established businesses included: two banks, three hotels, three attorneys, four general stores, two lumberyards, one candy store, and six churches in addition to the many other establishments. The town began to decline after the Great Depression, drought, and grasshoppers of the 1930s. (Courtesy Gregory County Historical Society.)

Founded in 1902, Bonesteel was named after an early setter, H.E. Bonesteel. In 1892, the town had been platted by the government but the lots weren't sold until 1900. (Courtesy Gregory County Historical Society.)

When President Theodore Roosevelt proclaimed that Gregory County was open to settlement in 1904, Bonesteel became the "Gateway to the Rosebud." Land seekers flocked to Bonesteel designated as one of the registration points for the land lottery. (Courtesy Andrew Qualm Collection.)

This photo by the train depot was taken 30 seconds after a shooting. The land rush to the Rosebud opening attracted many undesirable elements. The Battle of Bonesteel occurred when the town citizens drove the thugs out of town after a fight. (Courtesy Qualm Collection.)

The hotel and depot appear here as a 1914 winter scene on Christmas morning in Bonesteel. (Courtesy Doug Spitzenberger.)

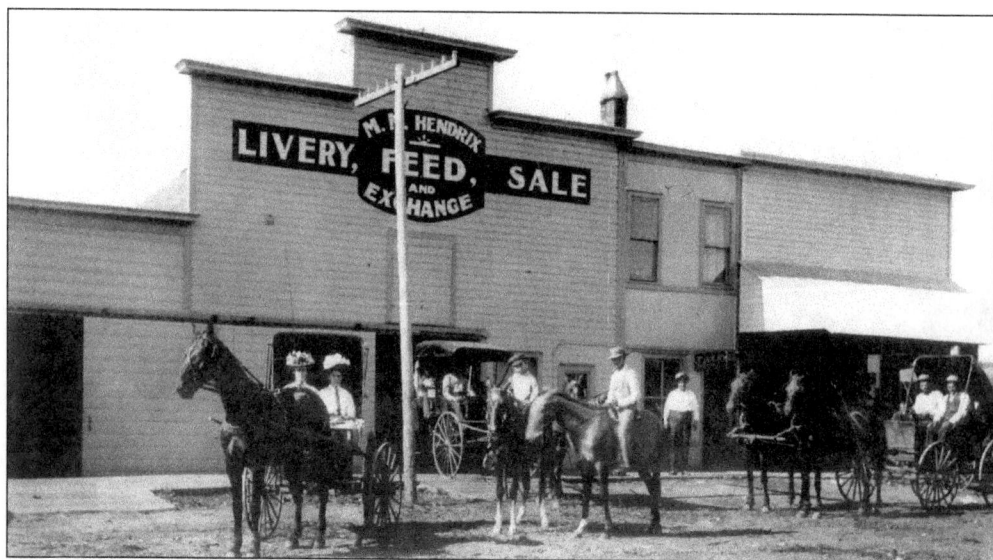

Two well-dressed ladies, to the left, stop for a snapshot on Bonesteel's Main Street. (Courtesy Andrew Qualm Collection.)

Three gentlemen relax in the shade of Bonesteel's land company. Apparently this was after the massive land rush. (Courtesy Andrew Qualm Collection.)

The town of Herrick was laid out in a perfect checkerboard pattern. By 1913, Herrick boasted of 62 business places. Among them were three livery stables, four general stores, three hotels, and three saloons. (Courtesy of Herrick News Subscribers.)

A train pulls up along the railroad water tank in Herrick. The depot and the three grain elevators stand trackside to the right in this 1910 photograph. An incoming train always aroused a flurry of excitement in a town. (Courtesy Herrick News Subscribers.)

The water towers, like the elevators and feed mills, were the tallest town structures. Almost every town had one. This 1907 tower stood in Herrick. (Courtesy Herrick News Subscribers.)

Herrick utilized the mall concept in 1917. This building known as the Zorba Mall housed several businesses including a dentist, Frank's Mercantile, post office, Doctor Stark's office, and an opera house. The building burned in 1924, leaving the adjoining wooden creamery structure untouched by the flames. (Courtesy Herrick News Subscribers.)

Many of the town saloons were decorated in ornate fashion as this one in Herrick. (Courtesy Herrick News Subscribers.)

Two ladies to the left, Helena Horst and Bertha Woflskeil, pose for a picture in the Herrick store owned by Sieler, Horst and Company. Jacob Sieler was Mr. Horst's brother-in-law and the "Company" was Bertha. Peter Horst took possession of the store in 1910. Subsequent owners of the store were Albert Anhorn, Melvin Duefeldt, Roger Kierstead, and Joseph Cerny who closed it in 1975. (Courtesy Herrick News Subscribers.)

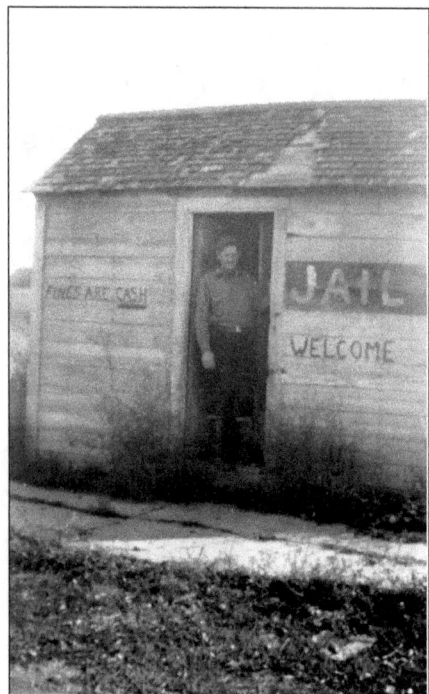

This Herrick jail appeared in Ripley's Believe It or Not as the only jail with a welcome sign. The jail was busy in the early frontier days and was later moved across from the dance hall where it was used from time to time for the rowdy clientele. (Courtesy Herrick News Subscribers.)

This photograph taken in the 1950s is of Herrick's town hall built in 1913. It was sided in sheets of embossed tin stamped with a brick pattern. The hall included the fire station equipped with a hose cart and modern chemical engine. The hose, cart, and axe were kept in a south room of the hall. A nearby city well provided the water. (Courtesy Herrick News Subscribers.)

On August 4, 1904, the land seekers gathered in the center of the Burke town site to line up for the race to claim their piece of land. The winners held their ground and marked their spots with stakes after the race and then filed. The railroad was built past Burke in 1907. Like Bonesteel, Burke had to clean up their town of undesirable elements. Burke became the county seat in 1917. (Courtesy Richard Papousek.)

In the early 1930s, Lake Burke was a popular spot. A beach house and outdoor facility were the first accommodations. The WPA and the CCC made improvements to the man-made lake in the 1930s. Ice blocks were cut from the lake in the winter and stored in icehouses. (Courtesy South Dakota State Historical Society Archives.)

Dr. Buchanan constructed a sanitarium often referred to as the Fountain Home or Buchanan Sanitarium. He built near a spring of warm water, which he felt had healing qualities. The home, located on Sully Flats, consisted of five stories with 49 rooms. After 10 years in practice, Buchanan sold the sanitarium because of ill health. Eventually the historic home was razed. (Courtesy South Dakota State Historical Society.)

Jack Sully built his ranch near the same springs that Dr. Buchanan would grow to appreciate. Jack had befriended Dr. Buchanan while driving a stagecoach from Yankton to Wyoming. When he learned that Sully was ranching in the west, he came to investigate and built his sanitarium. In 1904, a bullet from a deputy's gun killed Sully. The circumstances remain a mystery and the legend lives on. (Courtesy South Dakota State Historical Society Archives.)

Dixon began in 1904 when the Rosebud Reservation opened for settlement. Dixon served as a trading point for area settlers even though there was no railroad for miles. Bonesteel, Oacoma, and Platte were the only towns with railway connections, and they were about 50 miles away. The name Dixon, chosen for the new town site, came from Mr. Wilcox's birthplace, Dixon, Illinois. (Courtesy Richard Papousek.)

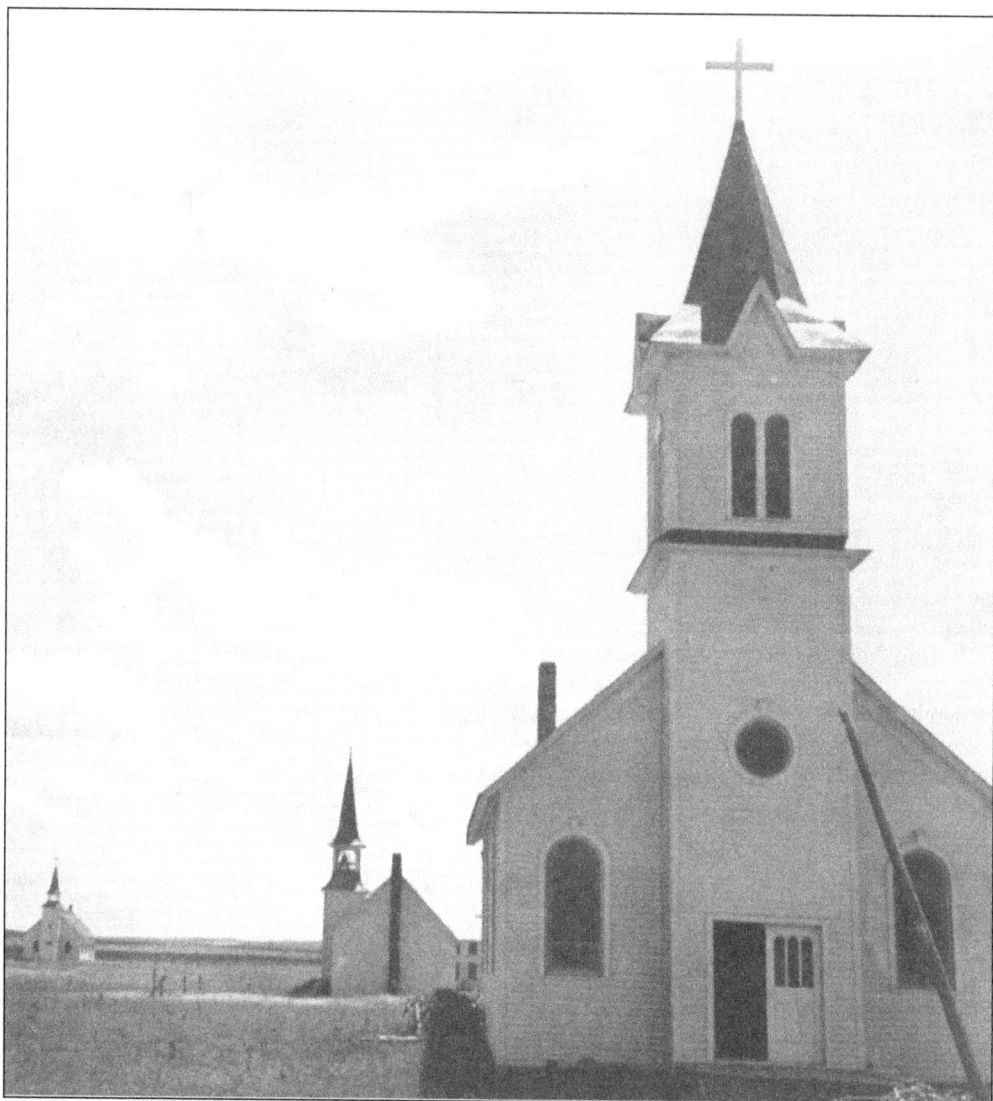

The Dixon Catholic Church commands the foreground in the photograph of Dixon's three churches. The Lutheran Church sits to the left and the First Baptist Church is in between. The windows of the Dixon School peek through between the two churches. The Lutheran Church was established in 1909. Tornadoes plagued the church several times, and it was moved to the south end of Main Street but unfortunately was unable to escape the tornadoes' curse. The Baptist Church, organized in 1908, burned in 1946 and was rebuilt in another location. The Catholic Church has been moved to the 1880 town east of Belvidere and the Baptist Church has been relocated to Dallas. (Courtesy Richard Papousek.)

Mr. Wilcox was one of the first settlers to the Dixon area. He built a store near the site of Dixon Dam where he traded with the Indians and white settlers. In 1905, M.D. Wilcox purchased lots in the new Dixon town site and moved his business to the new location. Area residents stand in front of the Wilcox store. (Courtesy Richard Papousek.)

At one time, Dixon had a population of about 100 people. Dr. R.V. Overton, the town's doctor and founder of the Dixon *Weekly Republican* predicted that, "No town on the Rosebud has the natural advantage to become commercially more important than our town." The combination of being an inland town, the drought and the Great Depression of the 1930s brought about Dixon's eventual demise. (Courtesy Richard Papousek.)

65

Mr. Wood built a hotel in Dixon soon after the town was established. The little community was proud of its two general stores, the People's Bank, drugstore, an implement business, a blacksmith shop, pool hall, hotel, livery stable, and doctor. (Courtesy Richard Papousek.)

The Dixon barbershop appears to be a busy place in this photo. Jessie Overton recalls her first glimpse of Dixon. "There were no roads on the section lines then so we approached Dixon on an angling road from the southeast. As we approached the town we could see a large building coming into town from the northwest. We learned it was to be the Dixon General Store. . . ." (Courtesy Gregory County Historical Society.)

When the Rosebud Reservation was opened to settlement on August 4, 1904, the founding of Gregory soon followed. The railroad reached Gregory in 1907 and by 1910 the federal census listed Gregory's population at 1,287. Photo *c.* 1907. (Courtesy Gregory County Historical Society.)

The 1907 Woolhiser Store was the first grocery and general store in Gregory. E. Woolhiser, the owner, became the first mayor of Gregory and served from 1908–1911. (Courtesy Richard Papousek.)

In 1905, 21-year-old Oscar Micheaux left Chicago for the Rosebud. He took over a relinquishment two miles southeast of Gregory and began homesteading. When he married his wife from Chicago, they relocated to a homestead in nearby Tripp County. Economic conditions worsened, and he returned to the East. Oscar wrote seven books and made 44 films, many with South Dakota homesteading themes. (Courtesy Richard Papousek.)

Richard Papousek of Gregory designed the re-creation of Oscar Micheaux's homestead. When Micheaux saw the land near Gregory for the first time, he wrote in his book, *The Conquest*, these words. "I gazed over the miles of it lying like a mighty carpet. I could seem to feel the magnitude of the development and industry that would replace the state of wilderness."

By 1909, Gregory, named for John Shaw Gregory, had grown into a bustling and prosperous town. (Courtesy Gregory County Historical Society.)

A road leads up to the backside of Gregory Buttes. Over the years, the town's people planted trees and established a city park at the base of the butte. (Courtesy Gregory County Historical Society.)

The buttes outside of Gregory not only served as a base for the town's water system but as a source of interest and entertainment for area residents. The Fourth of July fireworks display is set off from the buttes each year. The spectators are watching a community event on October 8, 1916. (Courtesy Gregory County Historical Society.)

Hopeful land seekers crowded the Gregory streets in hopes that they would be lucky and their number would be drawn at the land lottery for the opening of Tripp County. Fifteen regular trains arrived in Gregory daily filled with passengers. (Courtesy Richard Papousek.)

A grain-decorated hall was built on the north end of town when Gregory became one of the registration points for another land opening. Harry S. Truman registered here when Mellette County was opened in 1911. (Gregory County Historical Society.)

The Jackson brothers organized Old Dallas in 1904 in hopes the railroad would go through their town. When it became evident that the railroad might miss Dallas, Ernest Jackson made a trip to Chicago where he met with Marvin Hewitt, president of the Chicago and Northwestern Railroad to see if the railroad would link his town with the railroad line. After discovering that the railroad would not arrive, he and his brothers bought six-quarter sections west of Gregory to establish New Dallas. Photo c.1906. (Courtesy Richard Papousek.)

Originally, Dallas was located about four miles southeast of Gregory. Realizing in 1907 the railroad would miss their town, the residents of Dallas moved buildings to Gregory and Burke. The buildings were pulled over the frozen ground with horses. The men in the photograph are transporting the town's water system. After the Jackson brothers purchased the new town site, they moved the buildings they owned to New Dallas. (Courtesy Gregory County Historical Society.)

Dallas grew rapidly in 1907–1908 after its move from five miles west of Burke. The Jackson brothers initiated moving Dallas to a hill five miles west of Gregory where the railroad was due to arrive. Since Dallas bordered the eastern edge of Tripp County, it became the gateway and one of the registration points for the opening of Tripp County. In 1910, Dallas ranked in the top 30 towns in South Dakota with a population of 1,277. Photo c. 1908. (Courtesy Gregory County Historical Society.)

A passenger train arrives in Dallas in 1908. During the fall of 1908, the reservation lands in Tripp County were open for settlement. Between October 2 and October 21, 1908, 114,769 people registered at six registration points for the 6,000 available homesteads. Approximately 43,000 people registered in Dallas alone. (Courtesy Gregory County Historical Society.)

Dallas became one of the registration points for the Rosebud opening in Tripp County in 1908. An estimated 50,000 people came to register and many camped out in tents, as there were not enough rooms available. The registration forms were drawn out of a canvas bag after a prairie fire scare halted the proceedings. The drawing lasted for two days. (Courtesy Gregory County Historical Society.)

This rotary snowplow was necessary to keep the tracks open during the heavy winter snows. (Gregory County Historical Society.)

The cardboard lady welcomes customers to the Hafer and Wenzel Store in Dallas. The finest line of kitchen appliances is pictured. (Gregory County Historical Society.)

74

Five

HOMES ON
THE PRAIRIE

*We learned to love the old soddy, some of the happiest memories of my childhood
are centered there. . . .*

–Agnes Whiting

Some of the first homes on the prairie were the earthen lodges of the Arikara. The Sioux lived in shelters that could be taken down and set up in a moment's notice. This Lakota woman dries meat for the parfleches. (Courtesy Badlands National Park, Interior.)

Two cylinder Buicks were often used by the claim locators to chauffer the clients around the country. The autos were noisy and had to be pushed up the hills, but they were sometimes more convenient than horses. The land agent often carried a spade to dig up a sample of soil to show the client how productive the land could be. An especially cautious land seeker would return to the claim alone to carefully scrutinize the land without the agents input. (Gregory County Historical Society.)

Families were proud of the simple homes they carved out of the prairie. Agnes Whiting remembers her experiences in a soddy. "Each deep set-in window had a window seat and the west one was my favorite. Many, many hours I spent here, reading, sitting knees up, with my back against the wall. . . . The walls of our sod house were plastered and white washed. The floors were of rough boards. . . ." (Gregory County Historical Society.)

John Mysuph's 1902 homestead appears to be prospering with its frame house, barn, corral, and livestock. (Charles Mix County Historical Society.)

Edward Rubel, a French/German immigrant, drew a quarter section of land in the 1904 land drawing in Gregory County. When Edward was tragically killed on a trip to Chicago, his son Charles took over the homestead in 1907. The homestead has been in the family for 100 years. (Courtesy Richard Rubel.)

Father Charles, Brother Lawrence and Barbara stand in front of the 1904 Panek homestead. (Courtesy Gregory County Historical Society.)

Being able to build a frame house indicated an achievement of prosperity. Even though lumber was available with the arrival of the railroad, it was often expensive. (Gregory County Historical Society.)

This sod house was constructed with a wood roof, the most desirable of all roofing materials. (Courtesy Charles Mix County Historical Society.)

A 1913 photo of Mike and Katherine Schonebaum's 1892 sod and log residence was taken near Bonesteel. (Courtesy Andrew Qualm Collection.)

Severe blizzards often plagued the prairie with little to break the sweep of the blowing snow. The sod structure is practically obliterated by snowdrifts. (Courtesy Richard Ruble.)

This group of homesteaders is making a move to Tripp County after the second land drawing in 1908. (Gregory County Historical Society.)

Dan Shea drives his passengers over Ponca Creek on a special constructed bridge for autos. The Ponca Indians who grew vegetable crops along its banks, first occupied the Ponca. "Ponca" is a Sioux word for farms. The Ponca Creek begins near Colome and flows through southwestern Gregory County and empties into the Missouri above the Niobrara. (Courtesy Gregory County Historical Society.)

Prairie life was often difficult for women. However, many women wrote fondly of their home-steading experiences. One woman remembers in *Daughters of Dakota*. "I traveled all over the country, down to Gregory, Dallas and even as far away as Winner. I would take my bread that was to be baked or my washing and go over to the neighbors in my new buggy. It seemed it was more fun to have someone help with the work." (Courtesy Richard Papousek.)

Members of the Martin Skykora family stroll along a serene farm scene. The stone cottage in the background was the original Skykora homestead. (Charles Mix County Historical Society.)

This school built of sod was known as District 35 near Dallas. Settlers valued education for their children. Many schools began as sod structures. (Gregory County Historical Society.)

These children attended the Hawk School District northeast of Dixon in about 1934. Pictured, from left to right, front row, are: Delores and Martin Rezac; middle row: Louis Brozik, Margaret Grim, Marie Brozik, Betty Bailey, Jack Bailey, Cyrus Grim; back row: Ellen Bailey, Bertha Grimes, Doris Bailey, Teacher Mrs. Leekly, Jim Bailey. (Courtesy Betty Shaffer.)

Sod was used in the construction of this Lutheran Church south of Gregory. Early settlers established churches as soon as possible. When churches were not available, they held services in private homes. (Courtesy Richard Papousek.)

After establishing the towns of Old and New Dallas, the Jackson brothers, Earnest, Frank, and Graydon, turned their attention to establishing a ranch in Landing Creek Township in 1910. It was here that Earnest had acquired 640 acres on Five Mile Creek. The brothers purchased the already established Mulehead ranch from O.V. Kenaston. The Jackons also purchased the well-built Heggestad homestead for their headquarters. They then bought up more land from the homesteaders and began to build their empire. (Gregory County Historical Society.)

The Heggestad house is to the left of the photo. The Jackson brothers' big house is to the right. Barns and a two-story bunkhouse were added later. The ranch consisted of 160,000 acres, which ran thousands of white-faced cattle and employed a crew of 60 men before the Crash of 1929. The combination of the crash, drought, fire, anthrax, and low cattle prices forced the Jacksons to sell out. (Courtesy Andrew Qualm Collection.)

The following cowboys participated on the last round up on the Mulehead in 1924. Pictured, from left to right, are: Mr. Bear, Dutch LaFave, Jake Schemmer, Shorty Phillips, Charley Slater, Erhart Pepkie, Frances Turgeon, Archie Turgeon, Orr Unglaub, Fritz Schemmer, unidentified, Grant Smith, Hank Stamer, George Marty, Andrew Qualm. (Courtesy Andrew Qualm Collection.)

The cowboys of the last round up on the Mulehead are, front row: Herman Stamer, Shorty Phillips, Fritz Schemmer, Hank Stamer, Archie Turgeon, Jake Schemmer; middle row: George Marty, Mr. Bear, Ernest Jackson, Adolf Stamer, Graydon Jackson, Erhart Pepkie; back row: Charley Slater, Dutch LaFave, Orr Unglaub, Grant Smith, Frances Turgeon.

Six

BOUNTIFUL LAND

July and August meant threshing time. Something like thirteen to sixteen men of the neighborhood would help each other until each had his small grain in the bin. The women would cook three meals a day for the men.

–Helen Richter Lewis

Andy Osse breaks prairie near Dallas. With a team of three to four horses and a 14-inch plow, one to two acres could be broken in a day. The neighboring Carl Sundquist family relates a story about Carl plowing in the field in the Dallas History: "Carl was breaking prairie ground with a walking plow while wearing heavy, high shoes. He removed his shoes and walked barefoot behind the plow. After making a round or two, he changed his mind as he became aware of rattlesnakes becoming active after being disturbed by the plow." (Courtesy Gregory County Historical Society.)

Lewis Bouska plows for Andy McKenna in 1900. Lewis, his father Joseph, and brothers Anton and John came from Bohemia in 1893 and eventually settled near Wagner. (Courtesy Charles Mix County Historical Society.)

John Tulostos uses a riding plow to work a field near Dallas. (Gregory County Historical Society.)

Many more acres could be plowed in a day with the use of a tractor. (Courtesy Richard Papousek.)

Frank Tulustos harvests the 1915 bumper crop on his farm near Dallas. The men standing in the grain field proudly show off how tall the grain was that year. (Courtesy Gregory County Historical Society.)

Don Kimball operates a Farmall tractor while cutting the grain in 1929. Another man trips the bundles on the binder. The Kimballs bought the tractor from Gassen Implement in 1927. It was the first in Dallas Township. (Courtesy Gregory County Historical Society.)

Grain bundles were piled into stacks to await the threshing rig. Shocks would often deteriorate before the custom threshers arrived. (Charles Mix County Historical Society.)

The steam-powered rig was a definite improvement over horse-powered threshing even though it was a clumsy affair. Custom operators usually owned such tractors. A supply of coal and a water tank were necessary to keep the engine running. The steam engine had an exceptionally long drive belt as a safety precaution. Igniting the straw was always a possibility with the presence of the steam engine. Helen Richter Lewis describes the scene. "The children were thrilled to see that big steam engine pull in our field; with a separator attached and the big straw blower folded over its back as if to be resting." (Courtesy Richard Papousek.)

This photo is of the Brinkelson threshing rig from Geddes. A tractor operates this threshing machine. The separator tender stands on top of the threshing machine to oversee the entire operation. If it is a custom-threshing rig, the separator tender determines the farmer's bill by a weighing device. (Courtesy Charles Mix County Historical Society.)

Ed Kreeger poses for a professional photo with his young threshing crew. (Charles Mix County Historical Society.)

Threshing rigs made the circuit, harvesting grain for area farmers. This postcard appears to be an advertisement for the Ed Kreeger business. (Charles Mix County Historical Society.)

Harold Pavlis, standing in front of the threshing machine, was part of the crew that threshed for the Halva family in August of 1939 near Dixon.

A group of threshers pause for coffee and possibly sandwiches that are contained in the enamel dishpan. The horses in the background power the threshing machine. Threshing required many men to pitch and haul bundles with a team and rack to the separator, to tend the machine, to build the straw stack and to take care of the grain that came out of the spout. (Courtesy Charles Mix County Historical Society.)

Bill Morganfield's mother and stepfather, Mr. Culver, sell their produce in Dallas. (Courtesy Gregory County Historical Society.)

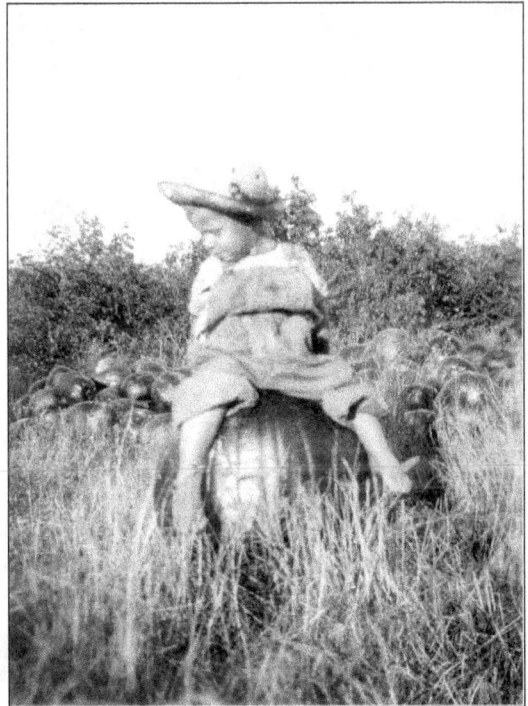

This young lad is not too sure of his Pumpkin perch.

Charles Rubel feeds his pigs on his farm near Dallas. (Courtesy Richard Rubel.)

Looks like supper to me! (Charles Mix County Historical Society.)

Men wait with their wagons to unload their grain at Gregory's elevator. (Gregory County Historical Society.)

These skyscrapers of the prairie appeared in every community. Each town had grain elevators to store grain brought in by the farmers until it could be shipped out by rail. Three different people owned each of these three elevators in Herrick. Only the middle elevator stands today. (Courtesy Subscribers of Herrick News.)

Dallas boasted three elevators as well. Boxcars stand trackside to be filled with grain. Doane-Sears Company, Mye Kenke Company, and Farmers Union Coop Association owned the elevators separately. (Courtesy Ruth Malone.)

During some years, the elevators could not accommodate the farmers' yields. The grain was then dumped on the ground as pictured here in Dallas. (Courtesy Ruth Malone.)

The year 1944 produced bumper crops. The Dallas elevators were practically buried in grain. (Courtesy Ruth Malone.)

A new concrete elevator, constructed in Dallas during 1948–1958, towers above the three wooden elevators. (Courtesy Ruth Malone.)

Bob Malone, who served as the manager of the Dallas elevator from 1930–1968, watches the scale. (Courtesy Ruth Malone.)

A new concrete elevator was erected in Dallas from 1948 to 1958 and was the second concrete elevator in South Dakota at that time. (Courtesy Ruth Malone.)

The land wasn't always productive. Tumbleweeds were the only vegetation that thrived during the dry years of the 1930s. Here, tumbleweeds were blown together during the constant dust storms. The tumbleweeds were used for feed when nothing else was available. Adding molasses to them made them more palatable to the livestock. (Gregory County Historical Society.)

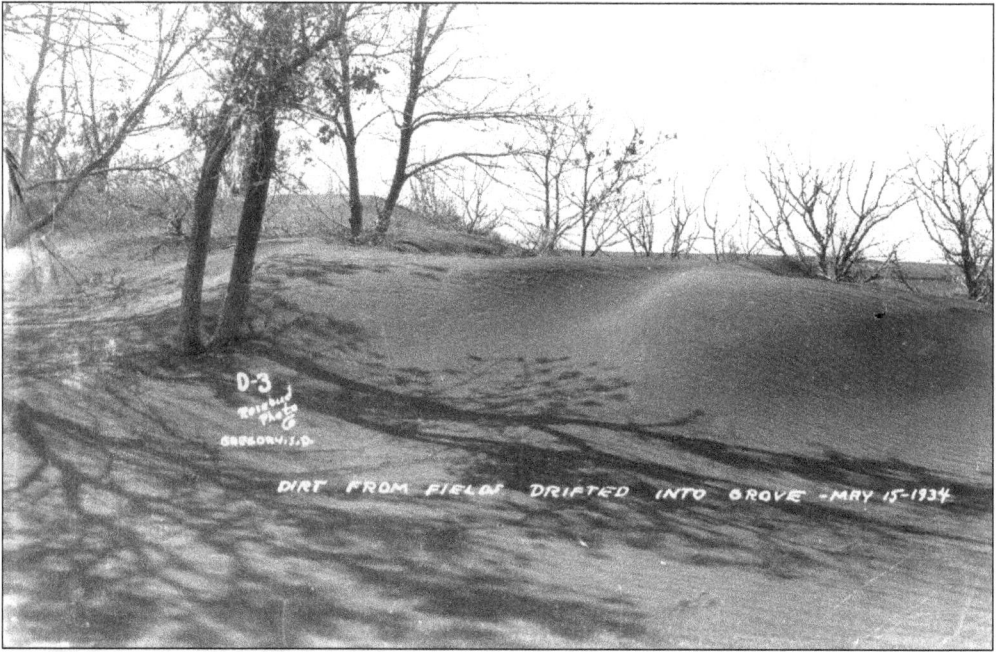

The drought and dust storms of the 1930s devastated the land and precipitated an economic depression that affected everyone for some time. (Courtesy Richard Papousek.)

Blowing dirt drifted into piles, covering machinery, fences, and buildings during the Dust Bowl era of the 1930s. (Courtesy Richard Papousek.)

Seven

COMMUNITY SPIRIT

We tried to meet each Saturday night to visit, play and sing. There was an intense spirit of friendly cooperation, when hard times came along, when a baby was born, and through sickness and death.
—Laura Belle Hegarty Schulze

Indian chiefs participate in a Labor Day parade in Wagner. The parade was one of the main attractions of Wagner's annual Labor Day celebration. Floats, decorated autos, horse back riders, Sioux Indians, and marching bands from surrounding towns supplied the entertainment. (Charles Mix County Historical Society.)

The Yankton Sioux were some of the main participants in Wagner's 1909 Labor Day Parade. Trains brought in people from the surrounding area to help celebrate in grand style. Approximately $1,200 was raised in 1910 to spend on the annual festivities. (Courtesy Charles Mix County Historical Society.)

The 1909 farmer's float appeared in the annual Labor Day Parade. Mr. and Mrs. Charles Ahrens decorated the float with shocks of corn, grain, milo, and orange pumpkins. (Courtesy Charles Mix Historical Society.)

"First Prize Flower Carriage, Labor Day Parade
Wagner, S. Dak., 1909"

Mrs. Harry James' flower carriage took first place in Wagner's 1909 Labor Day Parade. The carriage was decorated with yellow and white dahlias or mums accentuated by the pure white horse pulling the carriage. (Courtesy Charles Mix Historical Society.)

In June 16, 1910, an auto climb contest was held in Wagner. (Courtesy Charles Mix County Historical Society.)

This 1905 Fourth of July Parade takes place in Platte. Notice the row of grain elevators in the background. (Courtesy Platte Museum.)

Platte celebrated the Fourth of July with colorful parades. (Courtesy Platte Museum.)

A marching band leads a Bonesteel parade in this undated photo. (Courtesy Andrew Qualm Collection.)

Andrew Qualm and his friends are pictured with Canadian geese that they hunted on the Whetstone in the early 1950s. The Whetstone was a flyway for the geese. (Courtesy Andrew Qualm Collection.)

The arrival of the automobile to the frontier settlements inspired this auto parade in Herrick. (Herrick News Subscribers.)

Herrick commemorates the past with a historical parade on Main Street. (Herrick News Subscribers.)

Towns took pride in their water towers by painting them with the town's name and sometimes adding a design. Dallas' water town was included in Ripley's Believe It or Not as the only water tower in the center of a federal highway. (Courtesy Richard Rubel.)

Herrick celebrates the county seat festivities in this 1916 photograph. A float with two large flags appears in the foreground. A marching band follows. (Courtesy Herrick News Subscribers.)

Each town was proud of its sports program and supported their teams. Pictured in this Herrick basketball photograph are, front row: Herbert Horst and Joe Hudlicky; second row: Erwin Frank and Parker Ellston; back row: Carl Trautman, Victor Anhorn, Coach Ross Elliot, Kenneth Stracke, James Fortchner.

The Dixon square dance club, the Dudes and Dolls, were active for ten years. During that time, their dues bought the curtain backdrop and helped with other improvements for the Dixon Town Hall. Smoky Kratzer called the dances. (Courtesy Betty Shaffer.)

The Old Settlers' Picnics, held at the Dixon Town Hall in Dixon, were well attended for many years. (Courtesy Betty Shaffer.)

Mary Rewinkle, fourth from the left in the front row, owned the Dixon General Store along with her brother August. It was her privilege to ring the 1902 bell at lunchtime during each Old Settlers' Picnic.

Attendees at a Dixon Old Settlers' Picnic are, front row: Andrew Anderson, Emil Remter, Bertha Remter, Mary Jones, Mrs. Robertson, J.D. Robertson, Jake Ellwanger, Birdie Fenenga; back row: Frank Soesbe, Bryan McCollam, Colonel Hahn, unidentified, Mrs. Hahn, Eliz Zeller, George Lundberg, Marie Brozik, and unidentified. (Courtesy Gregory County Historical Society.)

Many communities formed bands for entertainment and participated in annual festivals. This brass band was from Gregory. (Courtesy Richard Papousek.)

A sleigh ride was often enjoyed during the winter months. (Gregory County Historical Society.)

The Bohemian Presbyterian Church in the foreground was built in 1928. The church in the background was built in 1904. Charles Mix County had the second highest concentration of Bohemians in the state according to the 1915 census. (Courtesy Charles Mix County Historical Society.)

Blizzards and winter storms were a threat on the prairie. Sometimes storms would often last for days or weeks. In town, the snow drifted in big banks in the streets. The town people worked together to clear snow in this 1915 photo of a Gregory storm. (Gregory County Historical Society.)

Eight

FORT RANDALL DAM

I got up and by the light of the moon observed that the sand had given way both above and below our camp, and was falling in fast. I ordered all hands on, as quick as possible, and pushed off. We had pushed off but a few minutes before the bank, under which the boat and pirogues lay, gave way. . . .
—Journals of Lewis and Clark

This June 1946 view looks downstream on the Missouri River before Fort Randall Dam construction began. Gen. Lewis A. Pick of the Corps of Engineers sponsored the Pick Plan that proposed a system of dams situated on the Missouri River where they would help with flood control and navigation. W. Glenn Sloan of the Bureau of Reclamation proposed reservoirs for irrigation and power. A compromise of the proposals created the Pick-Sloan Plan that would build four rolled-earth dams on the Missouri River in South Dakota. (Courtesy U.S. Army Corps of Engineers.)

Fort Randall was the first dam to be constructed over a ten-year period. This bottomland near Bonesteel was flooded after dam construction was completed. An early report by engineers concluded that the Mulehead Point, at mile 192.4 above the mouth of the Sioux River would be a good dam site. They estimated it would form a pool that would drown the flood plain for a distance of 45 miles. (Courtesy Andrew Qualm Collection.)

The Corps of Engineers mobile wash drill and crew extract samples at a 62-foot depth on September 11, 1947. As early as 1911, engineers examined the Missouri River and made favorable reports on the physical conditions for dam construction. (Courtesy U.S. Army Corps of Engineers.)

118

The contractor's drilling equipment is in operation at "Calyx" hole located in the vicinity of the powerhouse site. The diameter of the hose is 36 inches. Photo c. September 11, 1947. (Courtesy U.S. Army Corps of Engineers.)

The outlet works tunnels look northeast along the portal face. Concrete is placed in tunnel number four. Photo c. March 24. 1950. (Courtesy U.S. Army Corps of Engineers.)

A rivet passer places a rivet in a hole prior to driving on the construction of the powerhouse scroll case. (U.S. Army Corps of Engineers.)

Discharge channel plug number one shows flow of water over plug after blasting. Dredge begins the hydraulic removal of plug material. Tom Brokaw's father and grandfather worked on the Fort Randall Project and lived with the family at Pickstown, established in 1948 as a place for workers of the dam to live. Tom Brokaw tells of his experiences living there in his book, *A Long Way From Home*. Photo c. May 30, 1952. (Courtesy U.S. Army Corps of Engineers.)

"Western Chief" was a dredge used on the Missouri River near Pickstown. Tom Brokaw writes, "The residue from the dredging was forced out onto the flood plain at the river's edge; as soon as the water drained away, Warren and I would be on our hands and knees, crawling across the muddy landscape, looking for new treasures. We recovered buffalo skulls, Indian artifacts . . . and sacks full of agates and pieces of obsidian." (Courtesy U.S. Army Corps of Engineers.)

Workmen check weir surface with templates on the spillway. The spillway was a large as two football fields. Photo c. July 9, 1952. (Courtesy U.S. Army Corps of Engineers.)

The penstock section on a special cradle truck is being moved up tunnel one into place at the transition section. The view looks downstream on February 1953. (Courtesy U.S. Army Corps of Engineers.)

Riveting crew places rivets on a scroll case. Photo c. February 26, 1953. (Courtesy U.S. Army Corps of Engineers.)

A tainter gate for the spillway was shipped by railway flatcar to the job site in March of 1953. (U.S. Army Corps of Engineers.)

This low altitude view looks northwest and shows the downstream faces of the spillway and intake structure. Tom Brokaw describes the reaction to the dam building by area residents. "It was not unusual for families to drive to a vantage point above the river after supper and look down on the sprawl of construction and mighty earth-moving machines, working beneath bright lights, to rearrange the ancient landscape of chalkstone bluffs and bottomland." (U.S. Army Corps of Engineer.)

On September 15, 1953 a workman cleans the rocker base for the spillway bridge section, just prior to placement of a new section. (Courtesy U.S. Army Corps of Engineers.)

The paving operations show finishers preparing joint after surface finishing operations. Photo c. May 26, 1953. (Courtesy U.S. Army Corps of Engineer.)

This view shows the last section of the stay ring for turbine unit number eight being lowered into place on December 15, 1954. (Courtesy U.S. Army Corps of Engineers.)

A May 21, 1956 aerial view looks northeast showing all major features of Fort Randall Dam and reservoir. Portions of Pickstown appear at the right. Fort Randall Creek picnic and fishing area are at the lower left. Tom Brokaw describes the building of Pickstown. "I watched the hospital, the hotel, the church, and the school rise out of the leveled river bluff on which the town was constructed."

Shown is a June 27, 1956 aerial view of the project from approximately 5,000 feet. All major features of the project can be seen. (U.S. Army Corps of Engineers.)

South Dakota Governor Joe Foss is being interviewed for television prior to the dedication ceremonies on August 11, 1956 while others look on. (Courtesy U.S. Army Corps of Engineers.)

On August 11, 1956, South Dakota Governor Joe Foss delivered the welcoming address for the Fort Randall Dam dedication. He introduced the Representatives and Senators of the state also. (Courtesy U.S. Army Corps of Engineers.)

U.S. Senator Karl Mundt speaks at the dedication ceremonies. High voltage lines carried the power across the entire state of South Dakota. The first current was released in 1954. The R.E.A. cooperatives obtained the initial power that brought electricity to many rural areas that had been without electricity. The Oahe, Gavins Point, and Big Bend dams were then constructed to serve the rest of the state. (Courtesy U.S. Army Corps of Engineers.)

BIBLIOGRAPHY

Athearn, Robert G. *Forts of the Upper Missouri*. Englewood Cliffs, N.J.: Prentice-Hall, Inc., 1967.

Bakeless, John, Ed. *The Journals of Lewis and Clark*. Broadway, New York: New American Library, 1964.

Brokaw, Tom. *A Long Way From Home*. New York: Random House, 2002.

Gnirk, Adeline S. *The Epic of Papineau's Domain*. Gregory, S.D: Plains Printing Company, 1986.

Gnirk, Adeline S. *The Epic of the Realm of Ree*. Gregory, S.D: Plains Printing Company, 1984.

Gnirk, Adeline S. *Saga of the Missouri River Reveille*. Gregory, S.D: Plains Printing Company, 1982.

Gnirk, Adeline S. *The Saga of Ponca Land*. Gregory, S.D: Plains Printing Company, 1979.

Gnirk, Adeline S. *The Saga of Sully Flats*. Gregory, S.D: Plains Printing Company, 1976.

Micheaux, Oscar. *The Conquest*. Lincoln, Nebraska: University of Nebraska Press, 1994.

Wagner, Sally Roesch. *Daughters of Dakota, Volume I: A Sampler*. Carmichael, CA: Sky Carrier Press, 1989.